Health AND Fitness

Staying Safe

A. R. Schaefer

Heinemann LIBRARY

www.heinemannlibrary.co.uk
Visit our website to find out more information about Heinemann Library books.

To order:

☎ Phone +44 (0) 1865 888066

▤ Fax +44 (0) 1865 314091

▭ Visit www.heinemannlibrary.co.uk

Edited by Charlotte Guillain and Catherine Veitch
Designed by Kimberly R. Miracle and Betsy Wernert
Picture research by Elizabeth Alexander and Rebecca Sodergren
Production by Duncan Gilbert
Originated by Dot Gradations Ltd.
Printed in China by South China Printing Company Ltd.

ISBN 978 0 431015 34 7 (hardback)
14 13 12 11 10 09
10 9 8 7 6 5 4 3 2 1

British Library Cataloguing in Publication Data
Schaefer, Adam
Staying safe. - (Health and fitness)
613.6
A full catalogue record for this book is available from the British Library.

Acknowledgements

We would like to thank the following for permission to reproduce photographs: Alamy pp. 14 (© Vario Images GmbH & Co. KG), 21 (© Blend Images), 18 (© Gaetano Images Inc.), 27 (© Daniel Dempster Photography); Corbis pp. 5 (© Rainer Holz/Zefa), 12, 15 (© Hill Street Studios/Stock This Way), 28 (© ROB & SAS); Getty Images pp. 9 (Andrew Leyerle/ Dorling Kindersley), 11 (Peter Dazeley/The Image Bank), 23 (Joe McBride/Photographer's Choice), 26 (Imagemore Co. Ltd.); Jupiter Images p. 7 (Dynamic Graphics/Liquidlibrary); Photolibrary pp. 4 (Till Jacket/Photononstop), 10 (LWA-Dann Tardif), 13 (Image Source), 20 (Image Source), 22 (Plainpicture), 24 (Tips Italia/Hank De Lespinasse), 25 (Zen Shui/Michael Mohr), 29 (HBSS/Fancy); Science Photo Library p. 19 (Ian Boddy); Shutterstock pp. 6 (© Kristian Sekulic), 8 (© Cabania), 16 (© Ulga), 17 (© Thomas M. Perkins).

Cover photograph of a young skateboarders reproduced with permission of © Mike McGill (Corbis).

The publishers would like to thank Yael Biederman for her assistance in the preparation of this book.

Every effort has been made to contact copyright holders of any material reproduced in this book. Any omissions will be rectified in subsequent printings if notice is given to the publisher.

All the Internet addresses (URLs) given in this book were valid at the time of going to press. However, due to the dynamic nature of the Internet, some addresses may have changed, or sites may have changed or ceased to exist since publication. While the author and Publishers regret any inconvenience this may cause readers, no responsibility for any such changes can be accepted by either the author or the Publishers.

Contents

Some words are shown in bold, **like this**. You can find out what they mean by looking in the glossary.

Staying safe

Every day we do many different things in different places. It is interesting and fun to explore the world around us. But it is also important to make sure we stay safe.

Wearing a helmet when you ride a bike helps you to stay safe.

Staying safe means keeping away from **harm** or danger. **Protecting** your body and mind will also keep you safe. This book will help you to stay safe and have fun.

Always listen and watch carefully when an adult is explaining something to you.

Knowing important information

Knowing your address and phone number can help you to stay safe. One day you might need to tell an adult where you live. Maybe you will need to call your parent at home to ask them a question.

Learn your street address and telephone number.

You may need to tell an adult information to get their help.

It is good to know medical **information**. You need to know if you have any **allergies**. You should also know if you need to take **medication**.

Calling for help

Your choice:

Do you call 999 when someone makes you angry? Should you call 999 if you see someone who is hurt?

Speak clearly and answer the questions when you dial for help.

Only call 999 in a real **emergency**. Call 999 if you see someone is hurt very badly or if someone is in danger. Call 999 if you are lost or need help finding someone you know.

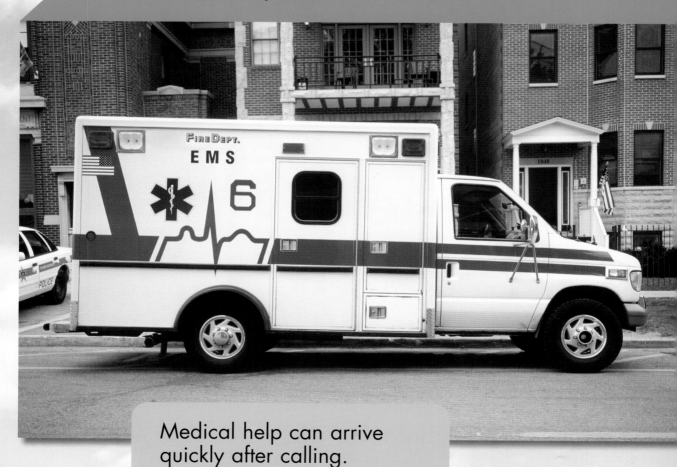

Medical help can arrive quickly after calling.

Who can you ask for help?

It can be hard to talk sometimes, but try asking an adult you trust.

Sometimes we all have problems and need help. Always start by asking someone in your family, a teacher, or a good friend to help you.

If you need help when you are alone, then look for an adult who can help you. Police officers, **lifeguards**, and firefighters can help you.

Do not be afraid to ask for help.

Staying safe in public

Your choice:

Do you often go to the park with your parents or friends? Is it a good idea to go off on your own?

Staying safe means staying with others.

12

It is important to tell your parents where you are going and what you will be doing. If you need help when you are out you can ask another parent or another trusted adult to help you.

You can have more fun with friends when you know you are safe.

Staying safe at home

Your choice:

Someone you do not know knocks on the door of your home and asks to come in. What should you do?

Sometimes workers come to your house to fix or check things.

Always wait for a parent to let a stranger into the house.

Never let a stranger in the house on your own. Keep the door closed and call a parent. The person at the door will understand.

Kitchen safety

You and your family cook and eat food in the kitchen. You should always be careful in the kitchen. The cooker can be very hot.

Stand back from the cooker when someone is cooking.

Do not touch harmful soaps or cleaning liquids.

Knives and other sharp kitchen tools can be **dangerous**. It is important not to play with these. Some foods and liquids can also be dangerous. Only eat or drink what a trusted adult says is safe.

Medicine safety

Your choice:

You feel ill. Someone offers you **medicine** with another person's name on it. Should you take it?

Is it ok to take other people's medicine if you feel ill?

Only take medicine that a doctor or parent has given you. Medicine that can help one person can hurt another. Do not take medicine on your own unless a parent shows you how first.

Some children use inhalers for asthma.

Safety on the move

You should make sure you are safe when you travel in cars. You should always wear your seat belt and stay in your seat.

Fasten your seat belt before the car starts moving.

It is important to keep your hands and arms inside the window. Putting your hand out of a moving bus or car is very **dangerous**.

Sit quietly on the bus, and do not throw things.

Safety on the street

Watch the signals and traffic before you cross the street.

People who walk, ride bikes, and skate share the streets with traffic. Always check the street for cars, lorries, and buses before walking, cycling, or skating in it.

When you are riding a bike or skating, watch out for cars. It is safer to cycle or skate with another person. Always wear a helmet and other **safety gear** and do not listen to music on headphones.

It is safer to skate in special skateparks.

Fire safety

Fires can happen in schools, at home, and in any other building. Stay away from fires and other hot things like cookers. Smoke from fires can also be very **dangerous** as smoke can make it hard for you to breathe.

Dial 999 if you see a fire in a building.

It is a good idea to know more than one way to get out of a building. Never take a lift during a fire. Always use the stairs.

fire escape

You should always get away from fires as fast as possible. It is a good idea to know where the **fire escapes** are in a building. Never go back inside a burning building to get something.

Water safety

Your choice:

The water in the sea looks calm. No one wants to go in the water with you. Can you go in alone?

Be safe in the water. Do not go in too deep.

It is a good idea to go into the water with an adult first. At the beach or the pool, make sure a **lifeguard** sees you before you go in the water.

Tell the lifeguard if you see someone needs help in the pool.

Safety for life

There are a lot of **rules** to make sure that children are safe. Adults usually follow these rules too. It is important for everyone to be safe.

It is safer to walk on the pavement and not on the road.

We all need to learn the **habits** of being safe. Living safely will help you stay happy and healthy for your whole life.

Healthy habits will last a lifetime.

Glossary

allergy when a person has an allergy, they get ill when they eat or touch a certain thing

dangerous something is dangerous if it can cause you harm or injury

emergency something serious where people need help straightaway

fire escape stairs on the outside of a building that you use if there is a fire

habit thing you do often

harm something that can hurt you

information facts that you can learn

lifeguard person who helps keep you safe at the pool or beach

medicine, medication things you take to feel better or stop being ill

protect when something protects you it keeps something bad away from you

rule instruction about what is and what is not allowed

safety gear things you wear when exercising to stop you getting hurt

Find out more

Books to read

Bicycle Safety, Sue Barraclough (Heinemann Library, 2008)

Busy Places: A Child Safety Book, Caroline Hardy (Mercury Junior, 2006)

Fire Safety, Sue Barraclough (Heinemann Library, 2008)

Safety Around the House, Ana Deboo (Heinemann Library, 2008)

Staying Safe on the Street (Safety First), Joanne Mattern (Weekly Reader Early Learning Library, 2007)

Your Own Safety (Stay Safe), Sue Barraclough (Heinemann Library, 2007)

Websites

www.safetycentre.co.uk/activities.html
The Safety Centre provides safety education for children. Find out how to stay safe, by doing these fun activities.

Index